PAUSE

A COLLECTION OF POEMS

ANANYA PESHKAR

Made with ♥ on the Notion Press Platform
www.notionpress.com

To,

"The people who made me feel seen when I thought the world was blind"

Contents

Contents

Prologue

Dear Reader,

This book contains 39 poems with a rollercoaster of emotions and complexities of circumstances that will make you pause and re-read it again and again and again. Now, why 39? why not 40 or 38? This reflects the idea of "almost" that is highlighted in my book a lot, almost won, almost enough, almost there. We try acheiving things in the perfect amount we forget It's enough even when It's not complete or full. Poetry has always been something that just flows in me like breathing, but as oxygen is important to survive so is poetry to me.

Your host for this journey

Ananya x

1. Last Page

Flipping till I find a page empty enough to write
It's filled to the top
With stains on the paper when I cried
You never cared
I almost died
I am done
Done with having you on the front of my life

Why did you have a knife?
I was the chapter of his book
He was the title to mine
Loving you was a crime
Jail was my home
Being with you was a job fulltime
Now I leave it empty
Just like you left me when I said I loved you
I close this book and I conclude I hate you
It to never be opened again
Like the grave
I let the words decay
You don't have a say.

2. Stranger

Become the person I hate and loathe
Or
Become the person in my dreams
Or
Become the person I share all my secrets to
Or
Become someone I see
Or
Become the love of my life
Or
Become the reason for my cries
Or
Become someone to me
Or
No one

Because,
I can't imagine the agony of recognising your laugh on a busy street
When the distance between us feels like a thousand feet apart
Locking eyes with the stranger who held me together as I crumbled
It seems the reason as I try to build up

Somethings just don't add up
My mind wont shut up
The only strange thing I see in you stranger
Are the eyes I could never forget

3. You

The one dimple that pops on your left cheek when you smile
The feeling when I get to call you mine
How you hate sushi's on a Tuesday night
134 freckles on your face
Your favourite Dior lipstick in shade so red
I know you hate the smell of cooked eggs
The perfume your dad gifted you in your closet
That one direction song you listen to repeat when you're stressed
That orange beaine your grandma gave you when you were 13
Your love for french fries over anything
I know you so deep
It's you who runs in my veins
I know you so purely
It's you who I pray to
It's you who I preach.

4. Anonymous

Every step outside my door seems like a thousand towards hell
I never had the courage to open your mail
I've still kept it in my old school bag
With our memories together sealed away
Sweet then bitter now
I knew you then not so much now
You're just another stroke on the canvas if my life
A stroke so dark I never expected it to be you
I have million words of mine to tell you
I've recited them in my diary like a prayer in the church
Like an addict to It's last blunt
I still act like I haven't opened that note
Who am I kidding it kept me afloat
It was never in that backpack and that backpack never hidden away
It sits proudly on my desk
As you sit in my heart
Secretly.
Anonymously.

5. Never His

I loved him
But he wasn't mine
He gave me his mother's pendant
But he wasn't mine
I promised myself to his heart
But he wasn't mine
We spent all night looking at the stars
But he wasn't mine
He told me he dreamt about us together
But he wasn't mine
He fell asleep on FaceTime hearing me breathe
But he wasn't mine
I knew exactly how many freckles he has on his face
But he wasn't mine
I belonged to him and him to me
But at the end of the day
He wasn't mine nor was I his

6. Hollow Words

I don't know what to believe
And what not to
It's all a show
Oh no
I interpret your signs as I'm taught to
Did you ever even love me or was it all fake?
Big fat emoji of a snake

Can't you see?
You're loosing me

See you say you love me
You say
And you say
Yet I seem to never be loved
You loved to love me but you never loved me
Nor did I feel loved by you

Love me
Please.

7. Broken Crockery

One broken piece
Two broken pieces
Three broken pieces
Four broken pieces
Slices slashes and leeches
It was a bad day
I was in a sour mood
I apologise I will Never do this again
I was angry I'm sorry
I will fix this broken crockery

8. Rukmani

To have,
to see the person you love take steps toward a direction you know you can't go in

To love,
to still love the person you cant hold

To believe ,
to still after everything believe in love that cant be acquired

A love so heavy with passion that it makes you float
To know every inch of a persons heart that it almost intervines your thoughts
To have a love as such?
so far away even the lords can't reach
But so deep ,even while hurting all you want is to crawl in that hole your forever resides in
Love is not calmness or happiness
Love is when your heart bleeds seeing them yet the only thing you want to do is
Bleed.
More.

9. It's Your Birthday

Blow the candles as I wipe my face
We don't talk anymore but I still remember this day
We weren't much
But something for sure
I force myself not to think about you but it makes me think about you more
Long gone those days where the clock didn't matter on the calls
I remember each detail
For sure I know you don't
For the first time
I'm okay with you not knowing
Because it made me know me
And that's enough
I was enough
I now let you go with the balloon in my hands
With the promise that evaporates
Of the drops that fell from my orbs in your name
No more
No more

Happy birthday x

10. Good Girl

I act like I'm okay
But I'm not fine at all
All those days I waited for you to call
Good girl always smiling
No tears in sight
Living in the hopes of might
Confused between what I knew and what was right
Hug me in front of them
Let me call you mine
You picked my peices
Glued them together
Just to break me like your promise
You had this of idea of me
I had to compete from your expectations
I begged for you to see
She was who you wanted not me
You wanted the perfect girl who didn't exist
It's me you wanted to fix
You fixed me just right
Just in shapes I couldn't bend
Through fights you knew I couldn't fight
I became your good girl at the cost of which I died

11. Let's Run Away

Lucky are those who love
And get love in return
Not everyone has the space to fit the dreams of their wedding

Some are born with this piece that shines like new obsidian
Black but bright
I long lost this right
I was ready to drop my life
You dropped my hand instead
I galloped towards dark
Why won't you hold me now?
We had a plan to begin a new us
But you ran away with my heart that I gave you on a silver platter
And now I'm left to lick the shame off the knife
The plan was for us to run away
And you ran away just right

12. When The Music Ends

Oh to have someone hold the tears a child carried
To know to love to scream
To hurt to heal to sleep
To stitch every scar with the kisses I need
To tangle to strach to please
To play that game to fold that crease
To breathe to loathe to feel
Pause.
Play.
Pause.
Repeat.
Bumps drag everywhere even in the backseat
It's your life
Drive rash or drive slow
Repeat the music or let it go

Pause.

13. Spider Under My Bed

The darkness darker than that of dried blood
The hushed crawling.
slowly I creep up to your neck
Weaving the thread under your bed
I see you sleep
Every corner in your room so steep
I slide off as I pounce on that baby fly stuck in my web
Landing beneath your shoe
Or so I knew
Am I filled with disgust or was it fear?
As for now I don't exist
Never did I really anyway
For you will never even find me in someone's memory
For I wasn't worthy enough of it
May you find that cobweb and destroy it
No one will ever know.

14. Mirror

I don't recognise the reflection in the mirror
The girl with bloodshot eyes and marks on her hands
I don't recognise the pathetic person I'm looking at now
But I remember those eyes
Oh the soft brown like the caress of a chilly wind on a sunny day
Like the fluffly blanket that's been with you since you were 12
It's there
But it's all lost in the maze of survival that little girl fought
Mirrors don't always show us whats the truth
But sometimes what we need to see
Like the little girl that resides within me
It's her I want to make proud
And I will

15. Million Lives

Got one but I've lived millions
From dragons to minions
I've had my heart ripped by the crushing love
From walks in the garden to getting lost in the grove
Small giggle when they hold hands
Long cries when they die
I've rode on horses and used guns
I've been a queen, a nobody and some
In this lifetime I've experienced a millions others
From the villains perspective or as a brother
Sometimes it was an escape from what was real and here
Sometimes I just wanted to be someone somewhere
I've been so many people I've forgotten who I actually am
Pm to Am
But It's okay
Because I think I was meant to feel and be a million things rather than one
Maybe my emotions couldn't only be filled like bullets in one gun
Maybe I was made for a dynamite of a life
Just Like this one

16. Addict (No Way Out)

Just One more drag
Just One more cut
Just One more kiss
Just One more chapter
Just One more drink
Just One more game
Just One more question
Just one more
What?
It's never only one more
It's never I'll never do this again
It's never just give me a chance
They will do this shit again
And you know it
And you will give them another chance
Why?
An addict will Never know.

17. ؟

Every night before diving in the abyss
One question haunts me
I retreat to my slumber
Fingers pointed at me
When will I ever truly be free?
Blink. Blink. Blink.
What if?
What if?
What if?
What if?
I wander, I don't remember
The excruciatingly painful beauty of being lost
You may discover a better world
But,
What if you don't?

18. Lost In Translation

I accept my mistake for believing a word that came out of your mouth
I forgot you're a man after all
Took the cursive for more than just that
And got hurt instead
I don't blame you now
I wanted the penthouse with your love
You locked me in the basement of your lust
After all I should've known better
You're a man after all
I preached to you like a sinner to gods
Maybe your love got lost in translation
Maybe I'm saying this so my pillow doesn't have to soak my tears again
Maybe it never existed in the first place
Maybe there was no love to translate
Not then
Not now

19. Bees

Here they come I say
As I hear that special ringtone under your name
Wings flapping tickle my insides
Time flies like lanterns in the sky when you're beside
I don't remember how or when
What changed from now to then
Strangers to something strange
Long hugs and slight stares
I still have something swirling in my deapths
Is it good I cant tell for I know you've changed
You break promises like porcelain
I'm afraid It's my heart next
Did you get my text?
Did you treat it like the rest?
The skeletons of butterflies I had for you churns in my stomach
Ouch
It stings
Buzz.buzz.buzz
Bees?
Butterflies?
Ouch
Bees.

20. Dollhouse

Glitter coated fingers
Pink lips that smile
Frilly frocks and fuzzy socks

Crawl

Show me what you drew baby
Why is it all grey?
Stare. blink.
What should I say?

Crawl

Mommy the dolls look so pretty can I braid their hair?
Keep them open like yours they look prettier that way
I touch my hair,
Grey.
Blink. run.
Mom? Can I braid the dolls hair?
Mom?

Run.

21. 9:59

Almost but never enough
The ink ends as im about to add the full stop
Tick
Tick
Blurred clock on my wall
Time is on a treadmill
Im about to fall
SOS
SOS
punctured tyres
Who do I call?
Who is it I'm trying to stall?
Tick
Tick
I push the brakes so hard
I look around
Almost getting away
Almost
Not enough
Shhhhhh
Is it 10 yet?
9:59
Almost

22. Locked door

Love was a room I kept walking into
but you shut the door in my face every time
When I found a new door you suddenly wanted to be mine
The scenic beauty overlooked by loud voices
My head spinns in directions I didn't even know existed
Why now?
Why not when you shut the door so tight even my tears couldn't seep in
Why not when I was shivering behind it you still didn't open
Why not when I pleaded and begged out in the open
You can't have me for when you want
When you didn't have me for when you had me
Now I'm so far the doorway
You want to be locked inside together again?

23. Middle Of August

Shade of red so deep
I almost took it as my heart
Green hue in your eyes between the brown
Gliding some dark in mine
Oh to the days your eyes used to shine
Date me
Or
Hate me
Or
Easily relplace me
But never turn the shade of black so deep
I might mistake it with the ink that bleeds the parchment
Yes the same one you gave me
Do you remember it?
I don't

What I do remember is you loved me
Now you don't.

24. The Snowman

Fluorescent glow from the fire burning beside me
Shadows creeping in like a sting
Cackling of the burn
I lean more into the snow embodied figure beside me
Water is slowly pooling beneath our feet
Hands interwined still
Warmth spreads in ones body
One melts like it's ink flowing from a quill
Why?
Why don't you just go outside I ask the now not so snowy snowman
Must you be with me?
Only to bleed?
His hands on my cheek stills my core
After all a soul like you is worth melting for
Drip.
Drip.

25. Autumn Roots

You fell in love with flowers that bloomed on my neck
I waited for you on the deck
But you drowned me instead
Soft and warm as you kissed them every day
You loved It's essence and its touch
My feet stayed glued to the ground
You were never around
You sleep safe and sound
While I'm lost in the crowd
You flew away with the summer breeze
Neglecting my roots
You never believed
Autumn rolled
With nothing sealed
The petals withered

You didn't know what to do
Neither did I

26. Oh Sweet Wanderer

Four walls in the colour beige
The picture from the photo frame staring upon me
I stare in the eyes
Hollow as ever
As what I expect from a sheet of paper
Forgive me I'm lost
They never told the route
The wanderer lost in the jungle of society with no maps
Please hold my hand that I seem to be drowning in my thoughts
Grazes of shame on my back as I dig my own grave
With no one to save
Love and was the only thing I craved
When I asked a question you looked at me like I was a clown
You're not here now
I keep sinking
Down

Down
Down

27. Puppeteer & The Puppet

Another day another song
The puppet dances with the delicate fingers of It's master
Tap
Tap
Tap tap
Tap
It's eyes filled with love for the person who helps him move
Control?
He sways to the rhythm of the bond that attaches him to his master
Strings?
When the puppet doesn't know It's life is controlled
It never will never not want the strings detached.

28. Little Girl

I bought myself a chocolate today
The one that she loved
When in a carnival
I search for her in the crowd
It's so loud
She was never taught how
But she fought like soldier just fine
No dolls in hand
Time flowing like sand
Knives were her friends
Never fit in so she was thrown out the box
At what cost?
Rollercoasters scare her
Along with that big bad man
Every night when she saw him she ran
The cold bathroom floor bought a peace the bed never did
She was used to it
Waiting for the hit
I bought myself a balloon
The same pink one she wanted
All she is a memory now
I will forever remain haunted

29. Cry Wolf

It's not what you think it is
(But it was)
Come on you're overreacting
(But I wasn't)
She's just a friend
(But she wasn't)
You lie like it's breathing
All you do is scheming
We didn't even start dating and you were leaving
I grieved a loss which wasn't mine for grieving
We've been through this road before
I'm already halfway the door
My heart bears the scars from falling down this hill
You went straight for the kill
You left me in the jungle of lies
Left me to root out what you said and what was once mine
You've cried wolf so many times
I don't think it's me you need to make Belive
I have nothing to greive

The wolf is here.

30. Lucifer

Not every black sheep has black skin
Some wear the coat of circumstance in the shade so dark
Blinding the morning star below the throne
Not every bad guy in the story is the bad guy
Change the narrative and find out why
Maybe we are the psychopaths
And psychopaths normal
Why do we die before we're dead?
Is the devil actually the devil
Or in reality he just had his own mind?
What people can't control people don't love
The devil doesn't come dressed in a black capes and red thorns
It comes in everything you think you know
But you don't
After all the devil too was once an angel
You too are an angel right?
Right?

31. Packed Suitcase

Another tear falls in the jar almost full
Full of promises you locked in my heart
The key packed in the suitcase you're taking
You packed my heart in between those fuzzy socks of yours
But you forgot to keep me
Locked in your arms
As you promised
But I knew you'd forget it long ago
I knew what I didn't wanna know
You held what you didn't wanna hold
I cried while I tried to seal my heart again
You sealed the suitcase
Was I so easy to leave?
Not for a second did you even freeze
Never looked back at me waiting
It wasn't only the promises you were faking
My heart wasn't yours for taking
You didn't care if I was crying or shaking
You had your suitcases packed long ago
It was only time till you decided to go
But it still hurt

much

much
Much more

32. Ugly Sunset

Shade of orange so dark
With red hue
I hate how it reminds me of you
I am wearing the hat your grandma sew
I started climbing with weight on my back
It seems to have been lost now with my crew
I don't know how
Alone on the hilltop
Do these voices ever stop?
Dark green leaves on the oak
That one unused road
I know where it goes
The sky is turning blue
In a shade I never knew
Every sunset is so pretty
Even the ones with cold dew
This sunset not so much
Because I'm not seeing it with you

33. Tarmac

Sprint on the tarmac towards me
Lift me up
So close It's your love I breathe
You
It's all I need
Let's go home
And do what we did on repeat
Fight
Eat
Sleep
Your touch is inked in my veins
Your love was so red it stained
Stained the sheets
Metal shone in your hands
I took it for a ring
There was no happily ever after
It was my back that bled
Akin to a snake your skin you shed
I happily ate the poisonous lies you fed
Memory so distant it seems miles away
Was it so hard to stay?
Hurt me slowly I could never fight back
Would I still wait for you on the tarmac?

Yes.

34. Alchemy

So what if you say I'm pretty
If the cost of it is starving every night
If you only like your house during Christmas
Everyday is a funeral
Nothing will ever feel right
The chain on my neck
Matches with yours like a mural
Your hand in mine
Till it slowly dies
My heart has bled a million times
With soundless cries
All the ties that were once mine
Dissolved with a shine that blinded me
Golden like the promise we both made
I hide behind the smile
No one did even try
To unveil the little girl behind
easy on the eyes
Little do you realise
Like the alchemy
There is nothing inside

35. Footprints

My feet bleeds from the footprints you told me to follow
What's done is done
But It's left me all hollow
Just like my smile
I wanna crawl and hide
I miss that slide
Or my childhood with greasy fries
So many unopened letters
You wanted go getters
Never enough
There's always a better
My hands bleed from begging your love
Push to shove
Burnt hands beacuse I never wore a glove
The distance like fire
I threw my dignity in
But it doesn't matter
It never did
It never will

36. Knives

Pain subsides as the wounds start to bleed more
Cuts all over me
Your hands in my skin like frost
Which one does hurt the most?
The skin heals but the hurt doesn't
Knife wounds heal
The ones with words doesn't
You were the hand that I reached for when sinking
You pushed me deeper
What's she gonna do?
Who's gonna need her?
I apologise for the trust in knives
Knives did I only trust
Atleast It's cuts were just.

37. Rewrite

Ink glides on the parchment
Creating lines never to be erased
No matter how many times I rewrite my side
You never seem to care
Hot honey eyes flash mine as I put a full stop
I erase it
Paragraph after paragraph
No clue what a word says
If only emotions were the pigment
That could stamp on our stories for eternity
Mind playing the invisible omition
Rewriting my scars
Cutting out my heart
With the bits of broken promises
Thoughts of midnight kisses
To sew the broken pieces
Only to brand it with a hot iron rod
With the words I never could rewrite
I tried.

38. Bury Me

I'm not dead but I may as well be
What would it take for you to see?
Didn't shed a tear as you buried me
I'm lost in the depths of your lies
Entangled with promises you never were willing to keep
Blinded by what If's and what it could've been
The grass was never green
I used to dream
More like a nightmare
I just screamed
I was talking day and night but you never heard
You flew away with the breeze of problems
The room is always brighter from the outside looking in
Now you think what it could've been
Call me and ask me where I am
I'm not dead but may as well be
Why are you here now
You buried me.

39. Take Me Back

The perfect house is crumbled now
It just happened I don't know how
The seeds I sow
They refuse to grow
I want to go back to being that little girl
The one who ran crazy with no care of the world
Who ate what she wanted with no calories in mind
She is getting harder and harder to find
I wish there was a button to shut off my mind
I am on my knees begging
No care in the world if they bleed
Please take me back
Take be back to the night I didn't have to cry
Take me back to being that little girl
Take me back to me

Just in another world

www.ingramcontent.com/pod-product-compliance
Lightning Source LLC
LaVergne TN
LVHW041254150826
845673LV00008B/2587

* 9 7 9 8 8 9 3 2 2 3 4 3 9 *